BEGINNER**UKULELE** **CHRISTMAS**CAROLS

Fifteen Much-Loved Christmas Songs Beautifully Arranged For Ukulele

DARYL**KELLIE**

FUNDAMENTAL**CHANGES**

Beginner Ukulele Christmas Carols

Fifteen Much-Loved Christmas Songs Beautifully Arranged For Ukulele

ISBN: 978-1-78933-373-2

By Daryl Kellie

Published by www.fundamental-changes.com

Copyright © 2021 Fundamental Changes

www.fundamental-changes.com

Over 12,000 fans on Facebook: **FundamentalChangesInGuitar**

Instagram: **FundamentalChanges**

For over 350 Free Guitar Lessons with Videos Check Out

www.fundamental-changes.com

Cover Image Copyright: Shutterstock – Africa Studio

Contents

Introduction

A Christmas sing-along was always a big tradition for my family. For many years we would noisily clang our way through pretty much any Christmas tune you could imagine and record our yearly Christmas "album" on what was once the height of modern technology... an 8-track minidisc recorder (don't I feel old?!).

As the years have passed, sadly so have many of our dear family members, but listening back to our old recordings and playing these songs helps us to connect and remember the wonderful Christmases we shared.

In this book I have arranged some of these timeless classics for ukulele. It's organised so you can begin with just a rudimentary understanding of the instrument and progress gradually as you work through each song.

This book will, of course, work well as a stand-alone resource, but can be used along with my other ukulele title *The First 100 Chords For Ukulele,* which delves into much more detail about chords and strumming patterns.

With just a few basic chords you will find that you are able to play a huge number of your favourite Christmas classics.

If you're a relative beginner at ukulele, work through this book in sequence, as new chords are added in each successive song. If you've got a bit of experience, then feel free to jump right in wherever you like.

Happy strumming and, indeed, *Mele Kalikimaka!* (Merry Christmas!)

Daryl

Get the Audio

The audio files for this book are available to download for free from **www.fundamental-changes.com.** The link is in the top right-hand corner. Simply select this book title from the drop-down menu and follow the instructions to get the audio.

We recommend that you download the files directly to your computer, not to your tablet, and extract them there before adding them to your media library. You can then put them on your tablet, iPod or burn them to CD. On the download page there is a help PDF and we also provide technical support via the contact form.

For over 350 free lessons with videos check out:

www.fundamental-changes.com

Join our active Facebook community:

www.facebook.com/groups/fundamentalguitar

Tag us for a share on Instagram: **FundamentalChanges**

1. Silent Night

Perhaps the most loved of all carols, *Silent Night* was first performed on Christmas Eve 1818 in the Austrian village of Oberndorf. The words were written by the young priest Joseph Mohr, and were set to musical accompaniment on guitar by Franz Xaver Gruber after flooding had damaged the church organ.

A ukulele accompaniment to this carol works beautifully and is fairly easy.

Begin by playing one of the easiest chords on the ukulele, C major. You only need one finger to play it.

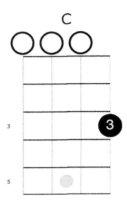

Look at how the above diagram relates to the fretboard. It shows that your third finger goes on string one at the 3rd fret. Use the tip of your finger and apply just enough pressure to push the string against the fret without it buzzing.

Hold down the chord and strum it slowly, playing one string at a time. Listen out for any buzzing open strings as this will mean that the underside of a finger is accidentally touching a string it shouldn't be.

The next chord is G7 and uses your first, second *and* third fingers simultaneously. Again, apply just enough pressure to press the strings to the frets, then pluck each string individually. Listen out for any buzzes and adjust your hand position until they've disappeared.

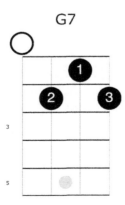

Practice switching between C and G7 for a few minutes and your dexterity will quickly increase.

Silent Night is in 3/4 time. This means that each *bar* (*measure* if you are in the US) of music contains three *beats*. You strum the chord once on each beat. 1 2 3, 1 2 3 etc. Try strumming the first eight bars. Use all *down-strums* (towards the floor).

Example 1a

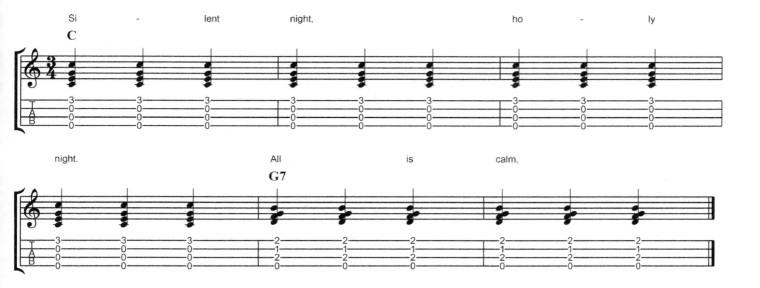

The next chord you come across is F major. To get to this from G7 is very easy, just leave your first finger on fret 1 and move your second finger over to the fourth string. Then simply remove the third finger.

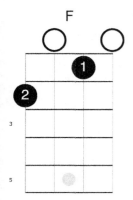

In bar eighteen you will see E7. For this, do exactly what you did for G7, but move your first finger over to the fourth string.

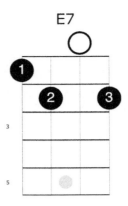

E7

In the last few bars, you will see the chords A minor (usually written Am) and D7. Am uses just one finger on the fourth string, fret 2. To get to D7 from here is very easy – just add a finger to the second string, fret 2!

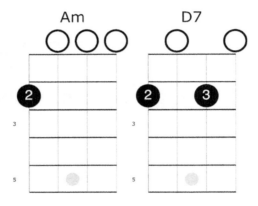

Am   D7

Now let's take a look at the full song...

Silent Night

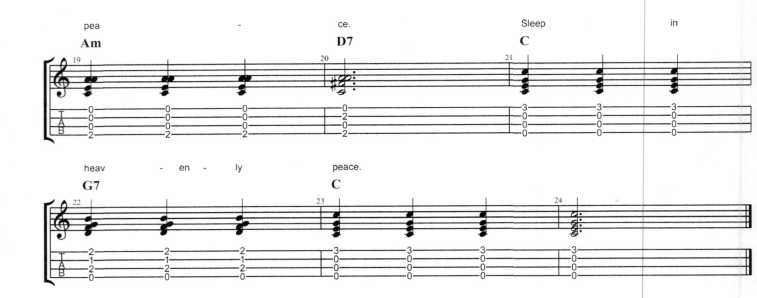

2. We Wish You A Merry Christmas!

We Wish You a Merry Christmas is thought to originate from the West Country of England. It was made popular in 1935 when Arthur Warrell's elaborate four-part arrangement was published.

This ukulele rendition uses the same chords as *Silent Night* with the addition of one new chord: Dm.

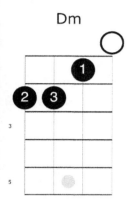

Combine it with the chord changes in bars seven and eight to help your fingers get familiar with the shape.

Example 2a

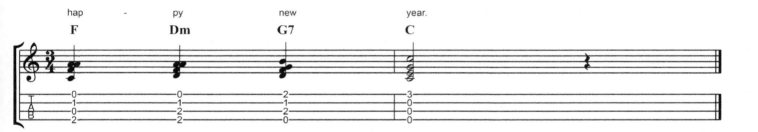

Let the C chord ring for two beats, then mute the strings for one beat, because of the 1/4 note rest that follows. Listen to the audio to hear how this sounds.

Example 2b

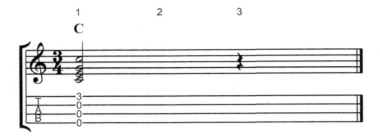

You can mute the strings by simply touching them with your strumming hand.

Now let's have a go at the whole song…

We Wish You A Merry Christmas

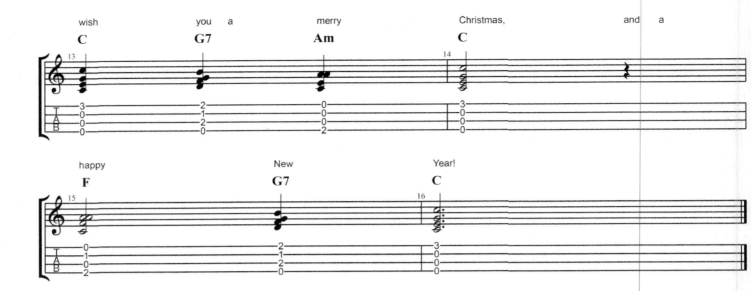

3. Jingle Bells

Jingle Bells was written by James Lord Pierpont and published as *One Horse Open Sleigh* in 1857. Originally intended as an American Thanksgiving song, it has since become synonymous with Christmas.

It uses another useful chord that you will often come across: G major.

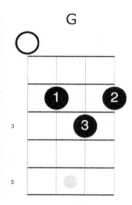

To begin, put your first finger on the 2nd fret of the third string, your second finger on the 2nd fret of the first string, and finally place your third finger on the 3rd fret of the second string.

Notice that the fingers make a kind of *triangle* shape. I found that remembering the finger shapes really helped me when I first started out.

Once your fingers are in place, pluck each string individually to check that the notes all ring cleanly. Adjust your hand position if you need to.

Next, strum this chord sequence, changing to C in the final bar. Count *1, 2, 3, 4,* for each bar as shown.

Example 3a

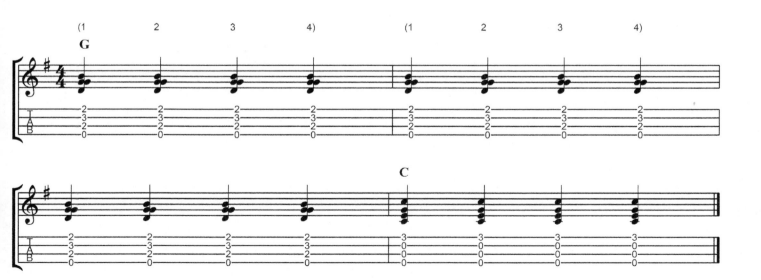

The next new chord you come across is D major. Notice how all three fingers fit into the 2nd fret. This might feel like a bit of a squeeze at first. Just make sure that the third finger doesn't touch the open string and stop it ringing.

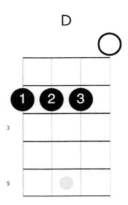

Practice changing from G to D a few times until you can make a smooth, quick change, allowing all of the notes to ring out.

The only other chord that you will need for this song is A7. This is very easy and shouldn't give you much trouble as it only uses one finger.

Place the first finger on the third string, 1st fret.

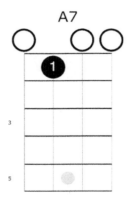

Right! Let's get playing…

Jingle Bells

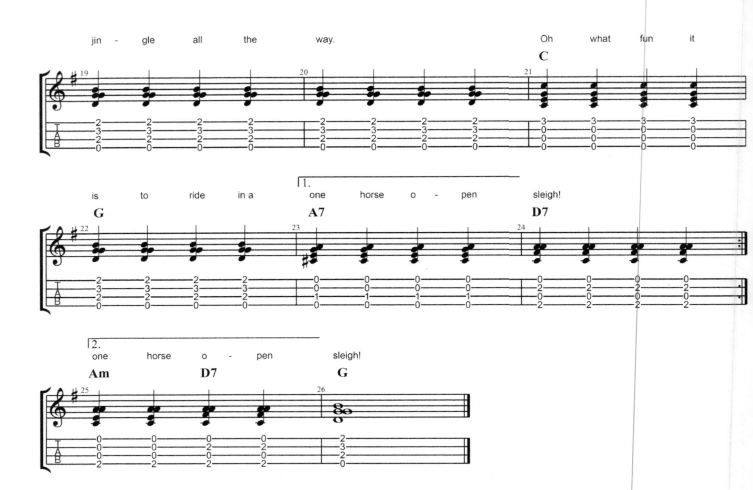

jin - gle all the way. Oh what fun it

is to ride in a one horse o - pen sleigh!

one horse o - pen sleigh!

4. God Rest You Merry Gentlemen

God Rest You Merry Gentlemen (sometimes called *God Rest Ye Merry Gentlemen*) is a traditional English carol dating back to the 16th Century, possibly earlier.

It is a great one to practice because it includes almost every chord we have learned so far. This rendition introduces the combination of both *down* and *up*-strums.

So far you are familiar with strumming like this, playing one *down-strum* for each beat of the bar:

Example 4a

To add more strums for added rhythmic interest, play the down-strum towards the floor just as you did previously, but now catch the strings on the way back up to play another strum in the gap between the beats.

If you do this on every beat, it will look like this (an up-strum is indicated by a V symbol).

Example 4b

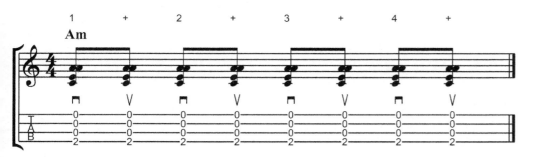

Count:

"One and Two and Three and Four and..."

If you count and strum together, then the *up* strums should coincide with the "*ands*".

Notice the symbols indicating the *down* and *up* strums? Look out for these in future, they're really important to make sure that rhythms are played smoothly and accurately.

The strumming pattern requires you to play a down-strum, followed by a down-up-strum as shown below You will count *"One, Two and, Three, Four and"*. Again, listen to the audio track to understand what this should sound like.

Example 4c

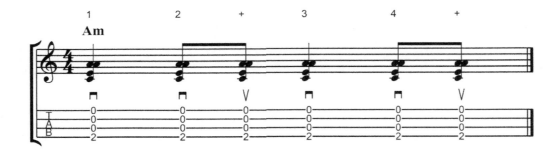

Once you have this new technique sounding clear and confident, try playing the full song…

God Rest You Merry Gentlemen

5. Auld Lang Syne

Auld Lang Syne is sung on New Years Eve all over the world. The phrase translates to *"for old time's sake"* and is credited to the Scottish poet Robert Burns.

The song features some interesting chord changes…

You'll need the chord G minor:

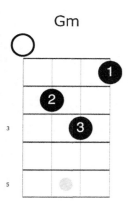

Also, C7, which uses just one finger on string one.

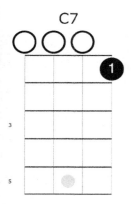

Plus, another new chord, F7.

For this, just play an F major chord and add your third finger to the third string.

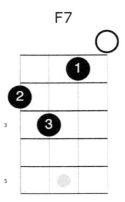

F7

The next new chord you'll come across is Bb (*pronounced B flat*), which is the first *barre* chord that we have encountered.

A barre chord uses a finger to make a bar across multiple strings. You'll see from the diagram that the first finger must lie across both the first and second strings.

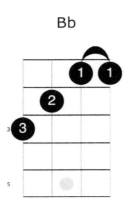

Bb

The great thing about barre chords is that they're *movable*. It's possible to slide a barre chord up and down the neck to play different chords, as they don't contain any open strings.

For example, if you slide the chord shape up one fret, you'll get a B major chord. Knowing this little trick can really save some time, rather than memorising lots of chord shapes!

The last new chord you'll need is C# diminished. Use the first and second fingers on the 1st fret.

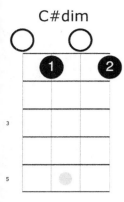

C#dim

Let's put some of these new chords together in *Auld Lang Syne*…

Auld Lang Syne

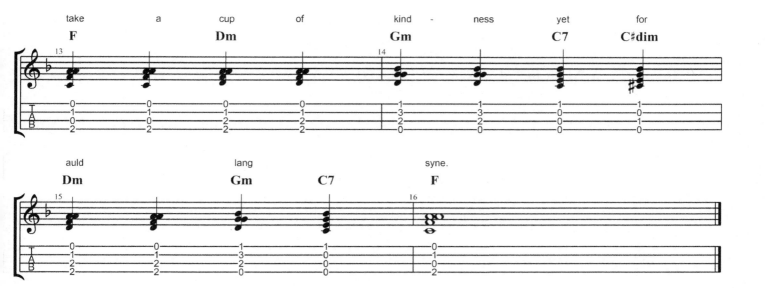

6. Deck The Hall

Deck The Hall is a Welsh melody taken from the 16th Century carol *Nos Galan*, which means New Year celebration. It literally translates to "first day of the month".

This ukulele rendition features a BbMaj7 (*B flat major seventh*) chord. It's similar to the Bb major but without the barre.

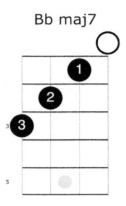

The strumming pattern uses both down and up-strums as shown in *God Rest You Merry Gentlemen*.

Count:

"One, Two and, Three, Four. One, Two, Three, *Miss."*

As you'd expect, "miss" means count the beat but don't strum the strings.

Example 6a

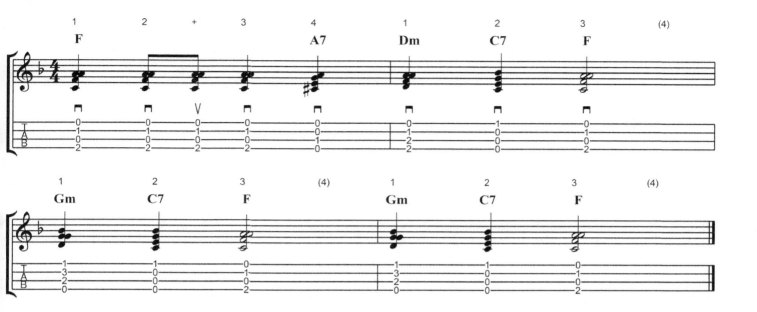

Now you can put it all together and have a go at *Deck The Hall*...

Deck The Hall

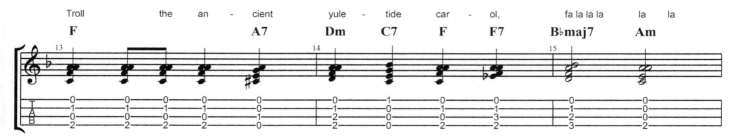

Troll   the   an - cient   yule - tide   car - ol,   fa la la la   la   la

F   A7   Dm   C7   F   F7   B♭maj7   Am

la   la   la.

Gm   **C7**   **F**

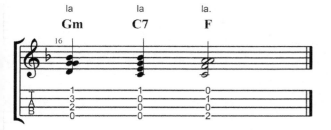

7. Good King Wenceslas

Good King Wenceslas is set to the 13th Century melody *Tempus Adest Floridum* (the time is near for flowering), which celebrates the coming of spring.

This ukulele rendition uses a couple of handy little tricks, allowing you to play some difficult chords quite easily.

In Example 7a, you can change to the new E minor chord from G major by adding one finger to string three.

Example 7a

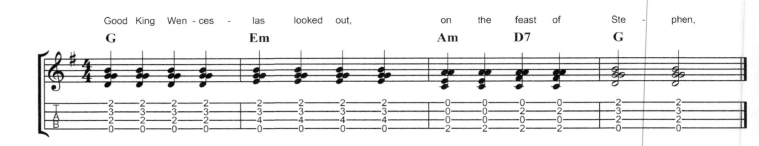

A similar hack for when you need to move from G to B7 is to use this D#dim chord instead of B7.

The sound is incredibly similar, but the shape is so much easier to play. Notice how it is basically the exact same shape as G, just shifted over one string.

Example 7b

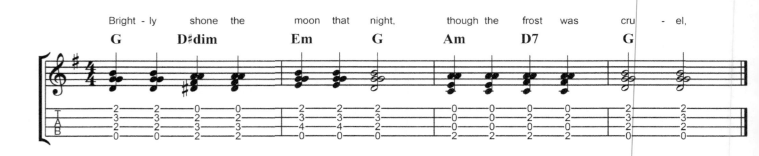

Something that might look a bit tricky at first is the bar with Cadd9, C, Am(add9) and D7. Despite their complicated names, changing just one finger at a time covers almost all of the chord changes.

Begin on the 5th fret (string one) moving to the 3rd fret. This gets you from Cadd9 to C.

Then slide to the 2nd fret and add a finger (also to the 2nd fret) on string 4. Now you have Am(add9).

Finally, move a finger from string one, to string two (2nd fret) and you have D7.

Example 7c

This kind of chord movement can really help to bring out the melody and we will include more of these in future. For now, have fun playing *Good King Wenceslas*…

Good King Wenceslas

8. Hark! The Herald Angels Sing

Hark! The Herald Angels Sing is a popular Christmas carol dating back to the mid-18th Century and uses a melody originally written by Mendelssohn.

We already know one *barre* chord, Bb, but here is another very useful one, B minor:

Bm

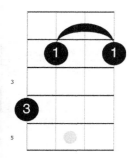

Notice that the barre needs to span three strings. It might take a few goes to get all of the notes clear. Remember to pick each string separately first to check they all ring clearly before you start strumming.

We have previously used a D# diminished instead of B7. This time I want you to use the full B7 barre chord. It requires a full barre across the whole neck and may seem tricky at first, but keep at it and you'll get there.

B7

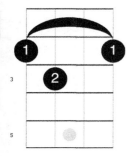

Let's try playing the song with these new barre chords…

Hark The Herald Angels Sing

9. O Christmas Tree

This popular German carol is based on a 16th Century folk song from Silesia, a historical region which now constitutes part of modern-day Poland.

This rendition uses the new B minor barre chord from the beginning of Chapter Eight.

The strumming pattern features some *down* and *up*-strums in 3/4 time. Count:

"One *and*, Two, Three. One *and*, Two, *Miss…*"

Example 9a

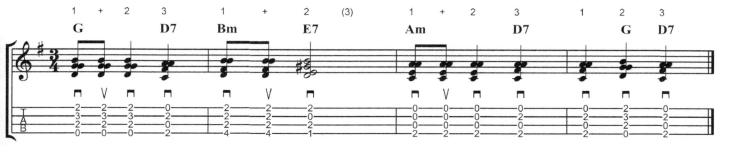

Now let's combine the many different chords we have covered in this Christmas classic…

O Christmas Tree

10. Ding Dong Merrily On High

Originally a 16th Century French melody written by the Composer and Cleric Jehan Tabourot, the English words were, in fact, added centuries later by George Ratcliffe Woodward.

This carol builds on many of the barre chords we've covered, as well as introducing a few new chords.

Here is Cm. Play it just as you would Bm but one fret higher (barre the 3rd fret instead of the 2nd).

Cm

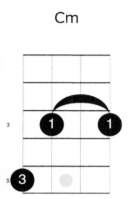

Let's take a look at the first part…

At first, the change from Fsus4 to F7 might seem challenging but notice that the first finger (which barres the first and second string in Fsus4) stays fairly still. Just pivot it up so that it only hits the second string, and move the second and third fingers into place.

Example 10a

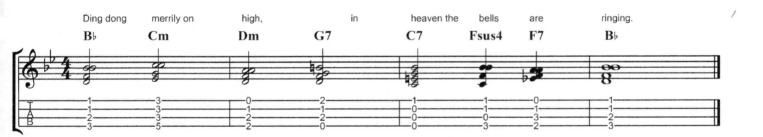

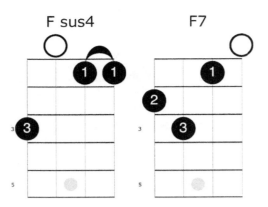

The only other change that might be a bit unfamiliar is Am7 to D7. But you can see here that they are very similar. The only movement necessary is the second string (3rd fret to 2nd fret).

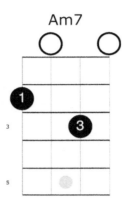

Once you have these transitions sounding good, have a go at singing and playing *Ding Dong Merrily On High*…

Ding Dong Merrily On High

11. The Twelve Days Of Christmas

Originally written without music in the 18th Century, *The Twelve Days of Christmas* was set to a traditional folk melody in 1909 by English composer Frederick Austin. The cumulative verses are thought to be French in origin.

This ukulele rendition uses almost exclusively chords we have dealt with previously, except for the addition of Csus4. Simply play the C chord as you would normally with the third finger on fret 3, but add the first finger to the second string:

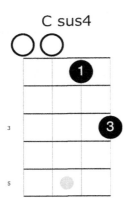

The only unusual thing in this carol is the odd time changes and repeats.

In bar seven, you'll see that the time signature changes briefly to 3/4 (three beats in a bar), then to 5/4 (five beats in a bar) in the following bar.

The first time you play this section, it will feel just like you are playing in the very familiar time of 4/4: the *first* beat in the bar of 5/4 functions as a *fourth* beat added to 3/4, giving a full bar of four beats. However… when you arrive at the end of bar nine, notice the instruction *Dal Segno*.

Example 11a

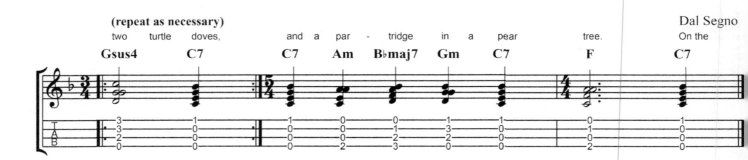

This tells you to go back to bar five (to the *Segno*, the *"S"* shaped symbol) and continue from there to play the 2nd verse.

Example 11b

Now, when you arrive at bar seven (the bar of 3/4), you will need to repeat it with the different words, "Three French Hens".

The next time, you will add another repeat of this bar, with the words "Four Calling Birds".

After this, you can continue to the next section, and indeed the "Five Golden Rings"!

I have only included the lyrics here for the first five days, but if you wish to sing the rest, just continue in the same way, adding a repeat to the 3/4 bar and the appropriate words!

Now let's jump in and have a go and this Christmas classic…

The Twelve Days Of Christmas

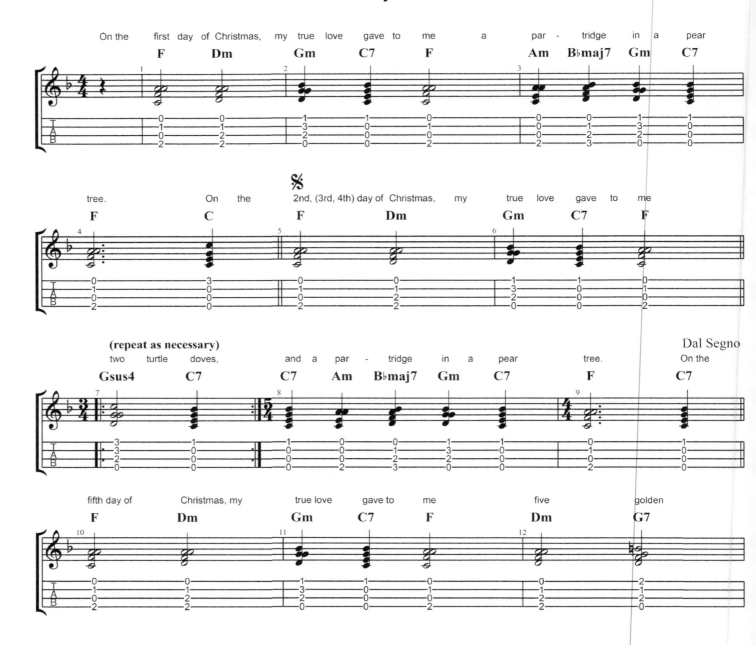

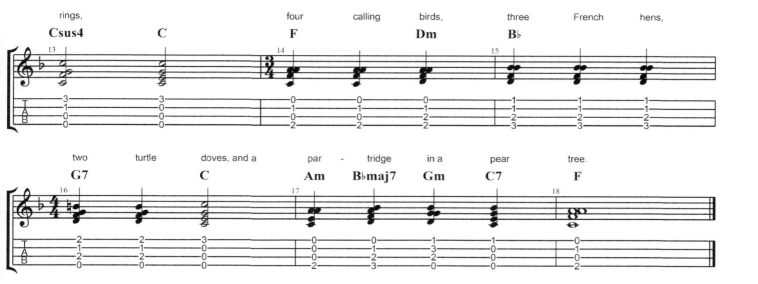

12. O Come, All Ye Faithful

O Come, All Ye Faithful (Adeste Fideles in Latin) has been attributed to many possible authors, including King John IV of Portugal. It is often credited to John Francis Wade (1711-1786), but this is likely an error. Wade worked as a copyist of manuscripts and his clients often requested that he sign his work due to his beautiful calligraphy. Like many carols, we may never know its true origin, but it remains popular to this day.

In this song we will use the fingers of the picking hand to pluck each individual string. This type of fingerpicking or *finger style* playing brings a whole new dimension to your ukulele accompaniments.

If you are new to this idea, begin with this simple exercise.

- Pick the fourth string with the thumb (labelled *p*)

- The third string with the index finger (*i*)

- The second string with the middle finger (*m*)

- The first string with the ring finger (*a*)

Example 12a

Here is the same approach on a G chord. Just hold down the shape and pick as before.

Example 12b

Once this is comfortable and the notes are sounding clear, try this while moving between chord shapes. Here is G to Em:

Example 12c

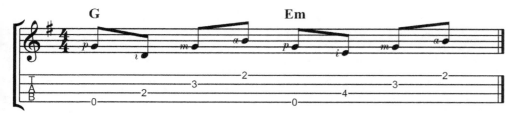

When you get to bar six, you will notice that you *don't* hold down a chord shape with the fretting hand. Pick the notes on the second string (fret 2, then 3, then 5 and finally fret 7) with an open first string after each. In the following bar return to the original picking pattern, then hold the strum in bar eight for two beats.

Example 12d

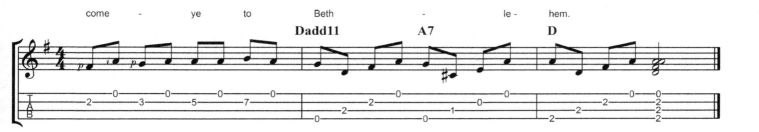

The only unfamiliar chord here is C6 which is the easiest chord on the ukulele!

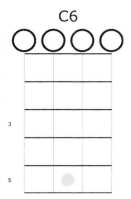

For Gsus4, just add your fourth finger to the first string (fret 3) when playing a G chord.

G sus4

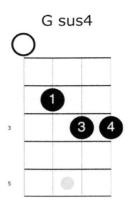

Now have a go at *O Come All Ye Faithful…*

O Come All Ye Faithful

13. Joy To The World

Joy To The World originated in the 18th Century. The words were written by Issac Watts and are based on Bible verses from Psalms and Genesis. It is now the most published Christmas hymn in North America.

This ukulele rendition uses a very useful movable minor chord shape: F#m.

F#m

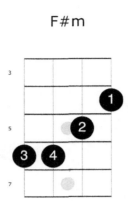

After the first few bars of sustained chords, there's a new fingerpicking pattern to learn.

First pick with the thumb (*p*), but use the other three fingers together to pick three strings simultaneously.

Example 13a

Have a few goes repeating this example until the rhythm is steady and even.

Once you are confident with the technique, try the whole song…

Joy To The World

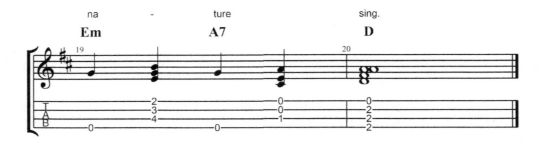

14. We Three Kings

This carol is credited to American clergyman and hymnodist, John Henry Hopkins Jr and its minor tonality creates a rather jaunting quality.

Until now, we have often used easier versions of Em and B7, but we will begin this ukulele rendition of *We Three Kings* with some fully movable versions

The Em is the same shape you used for F#m.

Em

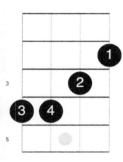

The B7 requires a full barre. Be sure to try each string individually to ensure that each note sounds clearly.

B7

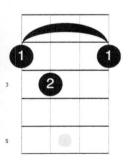

Now try those chords with this strumming pattern in 3/4 time.

Count:

"One, Two *and*, Three. One, Two *and*, Three ..."

Example 14a

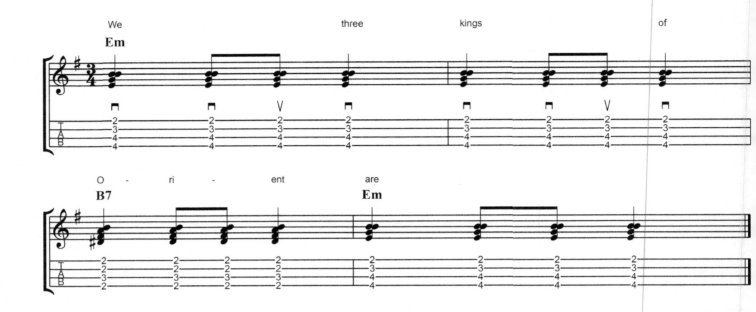

Soon after this you encounter Gmaj7 (*G major seventh*), which can be played by partially barring the first finger at the 2nd fret:

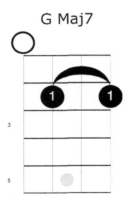

Cmaj7 is an easy chord with just one finger on the first string, 2nd fret:

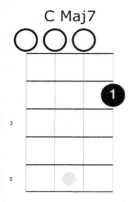

C Maj7

Next is a nice little trick with a couple of diminished chord shapes, both with an open first string. They are actually the same shape slid down a few frets.

Example 14b

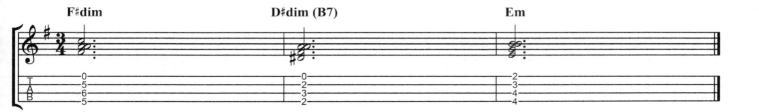

Once you can navigate these new chords, put them all together in We Three Kings.

We Three Kings

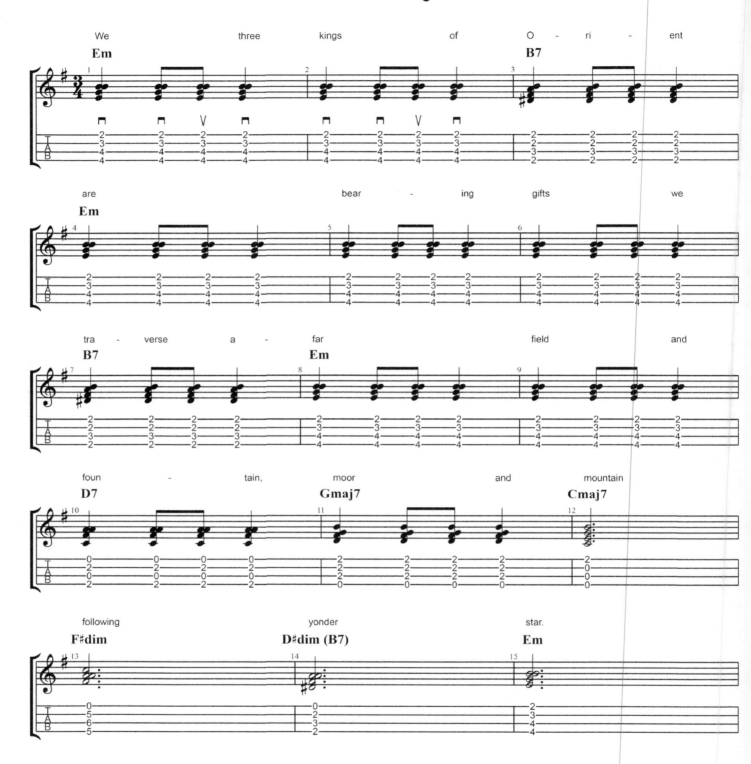

15. The Holly and The Ivy

The Holly and The Ivy is a well-loved traditional English carol. Its source is unknown but the symbolism of these enduring evergreen plants giving hope during the long dark winter is one thought to pre-date Christianity in Europe by thousands of years.

For this beautiful hymn I have included elements of the melody into the ukulele part, which means it works well as a solo instrumental arrangement.

Begin with a single open fourth string, then for the rest of the first part you will be able to simply strum.

Example 15a

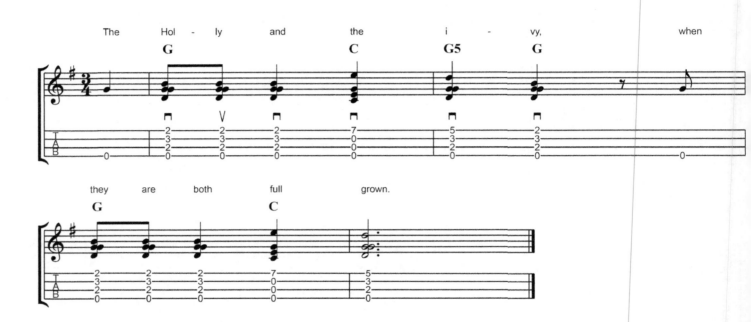

For this you will need a couple of alternative fingerings. C major with a finger on fret 7:

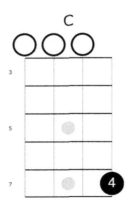

And G5:

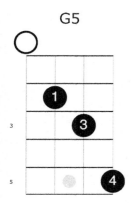

G5

In bar five, notice the curved line joining a note on the 2nd fret and an open string. This indicates that a *pull-off* should be played. Hold on the Em shape but pull the first finger down, off the note, towards the floor. It should "pick" the open string as it moves.

Have a few tries at this new technique until you can make a clear and consistent note from your pull-off.

Example 15b

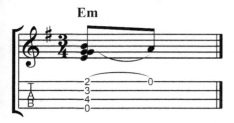

The final section includes a fingerpicked pattern followed by some strummed chords. You can swap easily between Am(add9) and D7, just change one finger from the second string to the first.

Example 15c

Now let's try the whole of *The Holly and The Ivy…*

The Holly and The Ivy

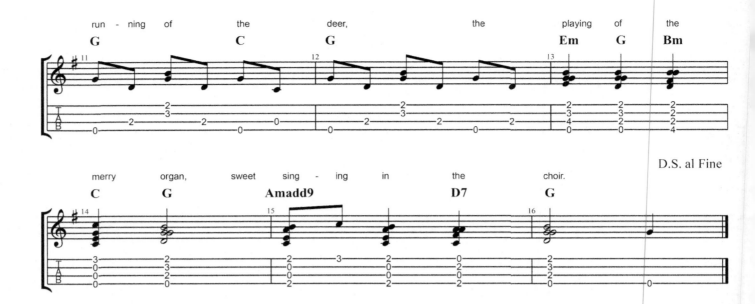

D.S. al Fine

Chord Dictionary

As I'm sure you've noticed from working through this book, there are many ways to voice chords on the ukulele. Here is a list of many of the common chords you are likely to come across in your future musical endeavours.

Enjoy!

C

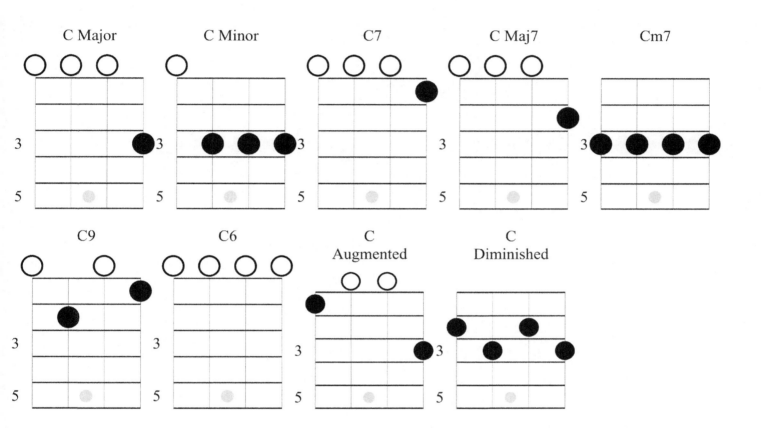

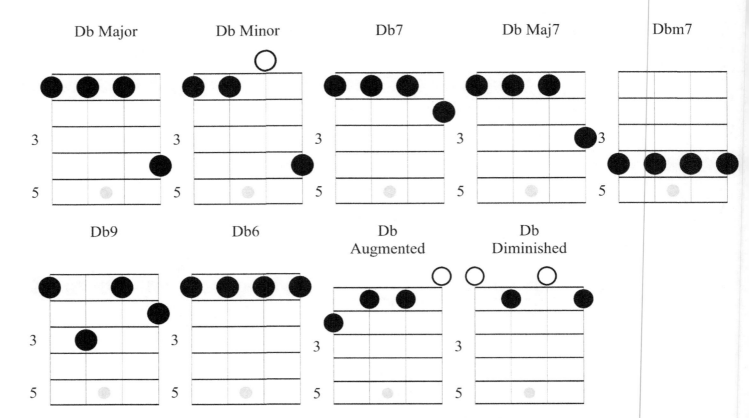

Db Major Db Minor Db7 Db Maj7 Dbm7

Db9 Db6 Db Augmented Db Diminished

D

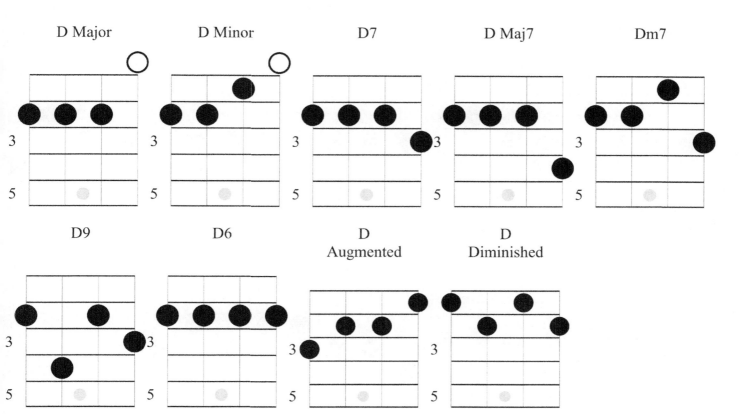

D Major   D Minor   D7   D Maj7   Dm7

D9   D6   D
                 Augmented   Diminished

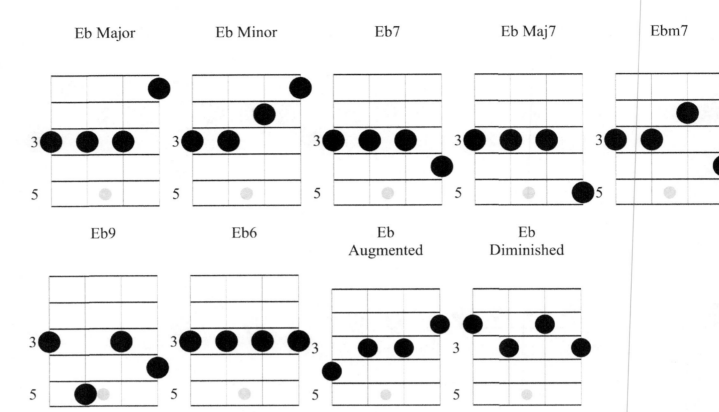

Eb Major   Eb Minor   Eb7   Eb Maj7   Ebm7

Eb9   Eb6   Eb Augmented   Eb Diminished

E

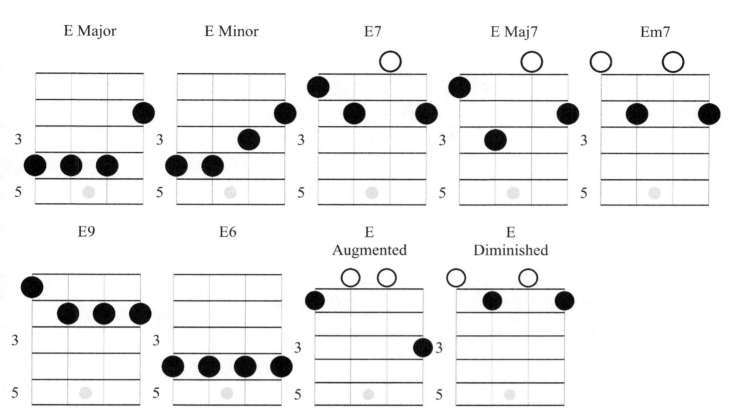

F

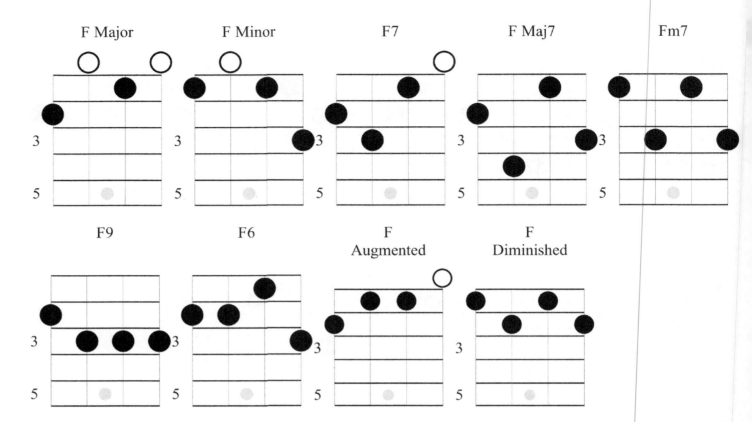

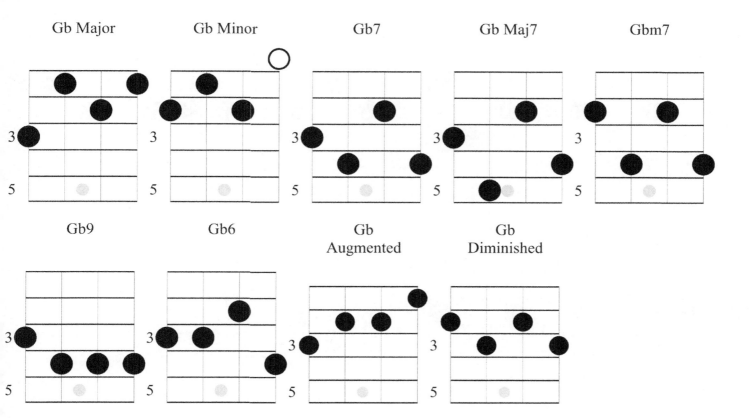

Gb Major   Gb Minor   Gb7   Gb Maj7   Gbm7

Gb9   Gb6   Gb Augmented   Gb Diminished

G

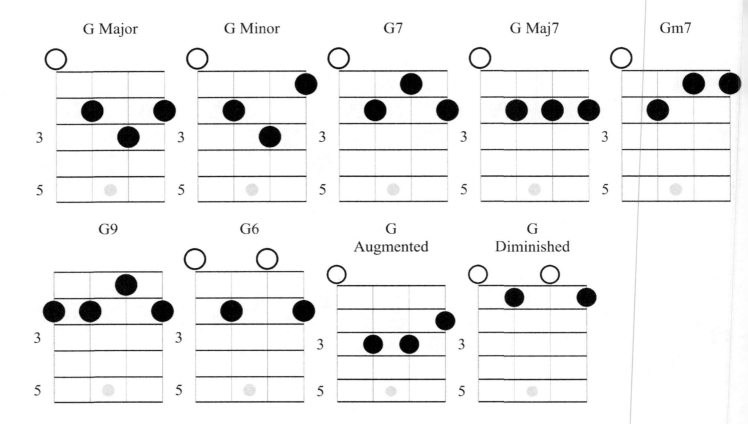

G Major   G Minor   G7   G Maj7   Gm7

G9   G6   G Augmented   G Diminished

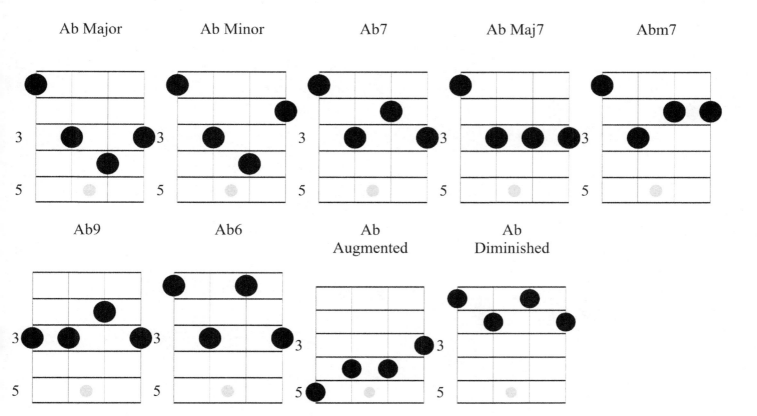

Ab Major   Ab Minor   Ab7   Ab Maj7   Abm7

Ab9   Ab6   Ab Augmented   Ab Diminished

A

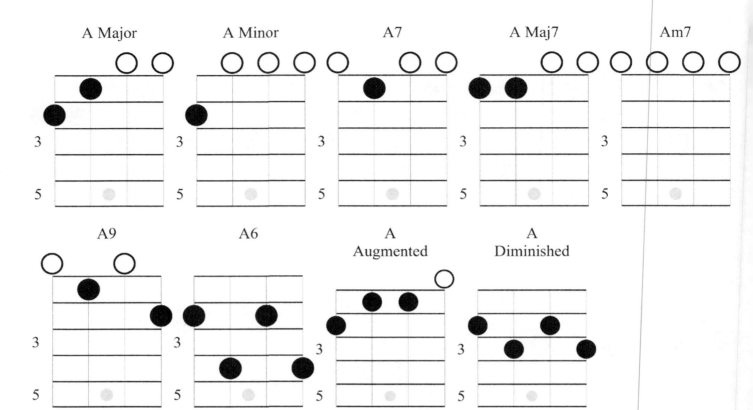

A#/ Bb

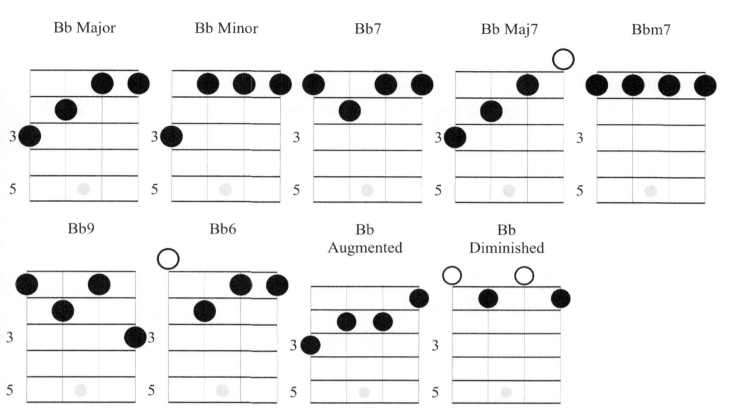

B

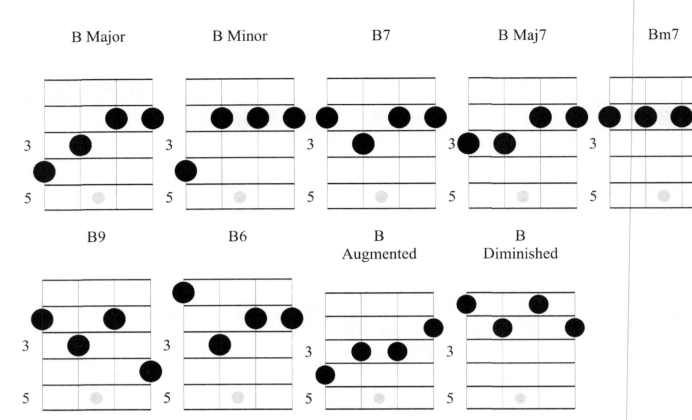

Printed in Great Britain
by Amazon

35691787R00044